PICTURED ROCKS NATIONAL LAKESHORE

Exploring by Trail and Shoreline

Autumn Jauck and Laura Pederson

Printed in Korea by Graphics International
First Edition

Dedication

I would like to dedicate this book to my sister, Andrea Chynoweth, who has always been an inspiration to me, and to my mother, Elaine Jauck, who opened my eyes to the beauty of nature all around me. - Autumn Jauck

I would like to dedicate this book to my parents, Bob and Linda, who guided me along life's trail and shared with me the wonder that is found in nature. - Laura Pederson

This book is also dedicated to the people of Munising and Grand Marias who share their backyards with so many who love adventures.

Acknowledgements

We would like to thank Pam Baker and Bill Smith, Park Rangers at the Pictured Rocks National Lakeshore for their advice, expertise, and assistance in the production of this book. We would also like to thank Youngsook Stibitz for helping out her friends in a pinch.

We would like to extend a special thank you to all of our friends and family members who have supported and encouraged us throughout this process.

Contents

Introduction

The name Pictured Rocks National Lakeshore is slightly deceptive as it conjures up images of pictographs and ancient carvings left as a legacy to the proliferate Native American Culture in this region. Many people come expecting to see pictures and diagrams engraved into the cliff's side. But Pictured Rocks was not created by a human hand. No, the force behind Pictured Rocks is something much older and more powerful. It is the result of wind, water, stone and minerals; the very elements of creation itself.

One could spend a lifetime studying the geology of Lake Superior and many books have been devoted to that subject. So we will not discuss here in depth the geological details. However, one cannot truly appreciate Pictured Rocks without understanding that the dramatic beauty we see today was created by millions of years of moving water.

Ancient glaciers moving through the area helped to shape the landscape. Layer by layer, century by century, sediment was molded into the cliffs that now tower 300 feet above Lake Superior. Crashing waves, ice, frost, and driving wind cut away at the sandstone escarpment forming the unique shapes we see today along the lake's edge. Streams from ancient inland lakes cut channels to the lake, and now provide us with magnificent waterfalls.

Minerals seeping through the porous rock give the fantastic colors that we see today. Copper creates the blue/green hue, manganese gives the black stain, and iron brings the rust/brown bleeds. These minerals, combined with the many layers of sandstone that vary in color from white, light grey, and cream color to dark red, paint the rocks in a kaleidoscope of patterns and even pictures if you look hard enough. It is this abstract art for which the lakeshore was named.

Pictured Rocks National Lakeshore is a large canvas on which nature sculpts and colors. It is a work in progress for the wind and water are still moving. Some changes are evident in our lifetime as stones fall and colors change. However, most changes are still thousands of years away.

This book is meant to give you a glimpse at the wonderful highlights to be seen but can in no way capture the true essence of the lakeshore. We encourage you to get out and explore. However, as with all great works of art, we hope you will treat Pictured Rocks National Lakeshore with the respect and dignity it deserves. It is truly a privilege to witness the process of creation.

By Trail...

Pictured Rocks National Lakeshore

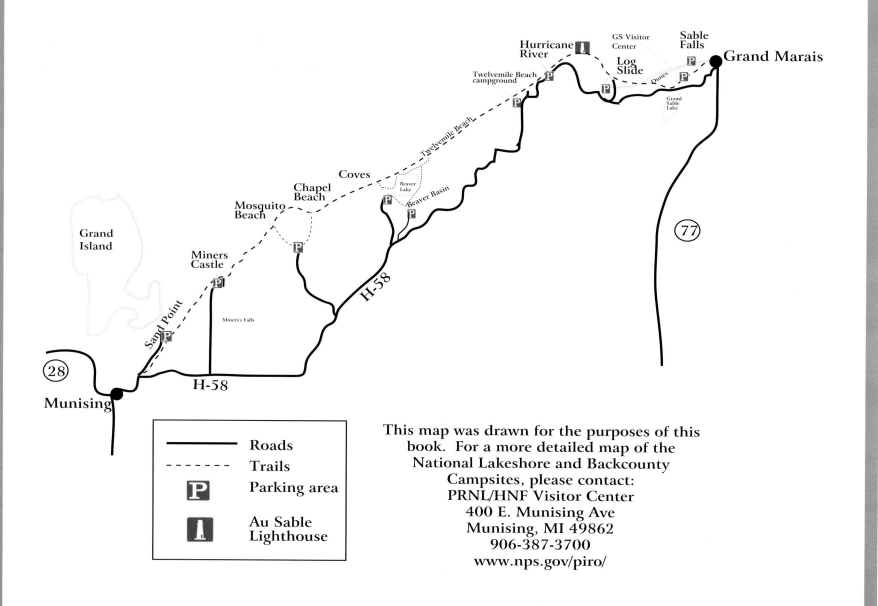

Grand Marais

Sable Falls

GS Visitor Center

Hurricane River

Log Slide

Dunes

Twelvemile Beach campground

Grand Sable Lake

Twelvemile Beach

Coves

Beaver Lake

Chapel Beach

Beaver Basin

Mosquito Beach

77

Grand Island

Miners Castle

H-58

Sand Point

Miners's Falls

H-58

28

Munising

	Roads
- - - - -	Trails
P	Parking area
	Au Sable Lighthouse

This map was drawn for the purposes of this book. For a more detailed map of the National Lakeshore and Backcounty Campsites, please contact:
PRNL/HNF Visitor Center
400 E. Munising Ave
Munising, MI 49862
906-387-3700
www.nps.gov/piro/

Sand Point

    Sand Point is a good place to start your excursion. Across the channel from Grand Island, Sand Point boasts a popular public beach sheltered from the harshest Lake Superior waves. This area is perfect for families who want to sunbathe, play and even swim. The shoreline is shallow for a long way out, and on warm summer days, the cold Lake Superior water is refreshing.

    On the back side of Sand Point, the beach is littered with large driftwood and rocks. From here you can see the Pictured Rocks Cliffs beginning to rise in the distance. A sand bar just a few hundred feet from shore provides a resting point for dozens of gulls in the summer. In the winter, Sand Point is the only point in Pictured Rocks National Lakeshore where the road is completely plowed and allows you direct access to the Lakeshore Trail.

Sand Point to Miners Castle

The 5 miles from Sand Point to Miners Castle takes you from the shoreline all the way up to the top of the bluffs. This section of the Lakeshore Trail is a long walk through the woods with very few glimpses of Lake Superior. The trail tends to be wet and muddy almost any time of the summer that you hike and the plant life is thick and dense and often grown over the trail.

However, if you can brave the mud and mosquitoes, you will be treated to some unexpected and sensational waterfalls. As you hike the trail, you cross dozens of tiny creeks which eventually come together and tumble off the cliff's edge. The size and volume of the waterfalls will depend on the amount of rainwater and snow run off. The most spectacular falls will occur in the spring but don't forget your bug spray!

Miners Castle

Miners Castle is undoubtably the most popular destination in the park. Easily accessible by car, the paved path to the main overlook is only a few hundred feet. A large wooden platform juts out from the cliff, giving you not only a fantastic view of Miners Castle, but also of the sheer sandstone cliffs and the startlingly clear green water in the cove beneath.

With a little extra effort, you can walk down to another wooden overlook placed directly on top of the castle behind the two large rock turrets. This platform gives you an excellent view of the lakeshore in both directions, as well as a clear view of Grand Island National Recreation Area straight across the channel.

The Miners Castle area also features a small gift shop and information center and public restrooms. Interpretive panels along the footpath provide information about the history and geology of the area.

Miners Beach

Just a short mile hike straight down from Miners Castle will bring you to Miners Beach, one of the most beautiful sand beaches in the Upper Peninsula. Bordered by rocky shoreline on both sides, Miners Beach feels like a private oasis. Also accessible by car, Miners Beach is perfect for anyone who wants to experience the feeling of a wilderness beach but is unable to hike long distances into the backcountry.

Past the protective shadow of Grand Island, Miners Beach is an exciting place to be when strong north winds push the waves to shore with a fury, crashing them on the beach and rocks. On calm days, Miners Beach is the preferred spot for kayakers to launch as they brave Lake Superior's cold waters for a unique view of the Pictured Rocks shoreline.

Nestled in the towering red pines just above the beach are several excellent picnic areas, complete with tables and grills. There is a pit toilet available in the picnic area but you will need to bring your own water. The Lakeshore Trail also runs along the ridge above the beach through the woods. This area is always abundant with blueberries in the late summer.

About a mile and a half inland from Miners Beach is Miners Falls. Also easily accessible by car, the walk to the falls is less than a mile from the parking area. Miners Falls is one of the largest and most spectacular in the park. This hike is also one of the best places to view wildflowers in the spring, so numerous in this section that their heady perfume fills the air.

Miners Beach

As you leave Miners Beach, the Lakeshore Trail climbs up through a mixed conifer and hardwood forest and then winds along the top of the Pictured Rocks cliff escarpments. This 3.5 mile hike is well worth the effort because of the magnificent views of Lake Superior and the Pictured Rocks shoreline.

Mosquito Beach is one of the most popular backcounty beaches because in addition to a beautiful sandy beach, it also has rocky shoals that stretch far out into the lake. On the east side of the beach flows the Mosquito River. The river's temperatures are usually warmer than Lake Superior, and is a popular place for fishing or wading.

Mosquito Beach can be reached by an alternate trail leaving from the Chapel Trailhead. This 2 mile trail not only allows easier access to the beach but takes you past the lively Mosquito Falls.

Mosquito Beach to Chapel Beach

The Trail from Mosquito Beach to Chapel Beach is 4 miles of the most spectacular vistas Pictured Rocks has to offer. The Lakeshore Trail takes you up along the cliff's edge, over Grand Portal Point and then down again to magical Chapel Beach.

The main trail winds through the woods but stays very close to the Lake so there are many overlooks on the edge where you can look straight down and see the jagged rocks below. There are also fabulous views of the shoreline and glimpses of many rock formations such as Indian Head.

Probably the most memorable overlook of all takes you out on top of Grand Portal, a large rock formation that juts out into Lake Superior. Here you can walk along a wide expanse of rock with stunning views on all sides. Often you can view the Pictured Rocks Boat Cruises below as their passengers wave up at you.

There is much to explore in this section of the Lakeshore Trail so be sure to allow yourself extra time to see everything.

At the east end of Chapel Beach stands Chapel Rock. A magnificent lone white pine has perched on this rock fragment for over 100 years, weathering storms and wind. Its roots stretch across space to the soil on the rocks behind it, a lifeline of nutrients. It is one of the many marvels of Pictured Rocks.

Chapel Rock and Beach can also be reached by an alternate trail from the Chapel Trailhead. This 3 mile trail takes you past the stunning Chapel Falls as it thunders to the forest floor.

23

Chapel Beach to Coves

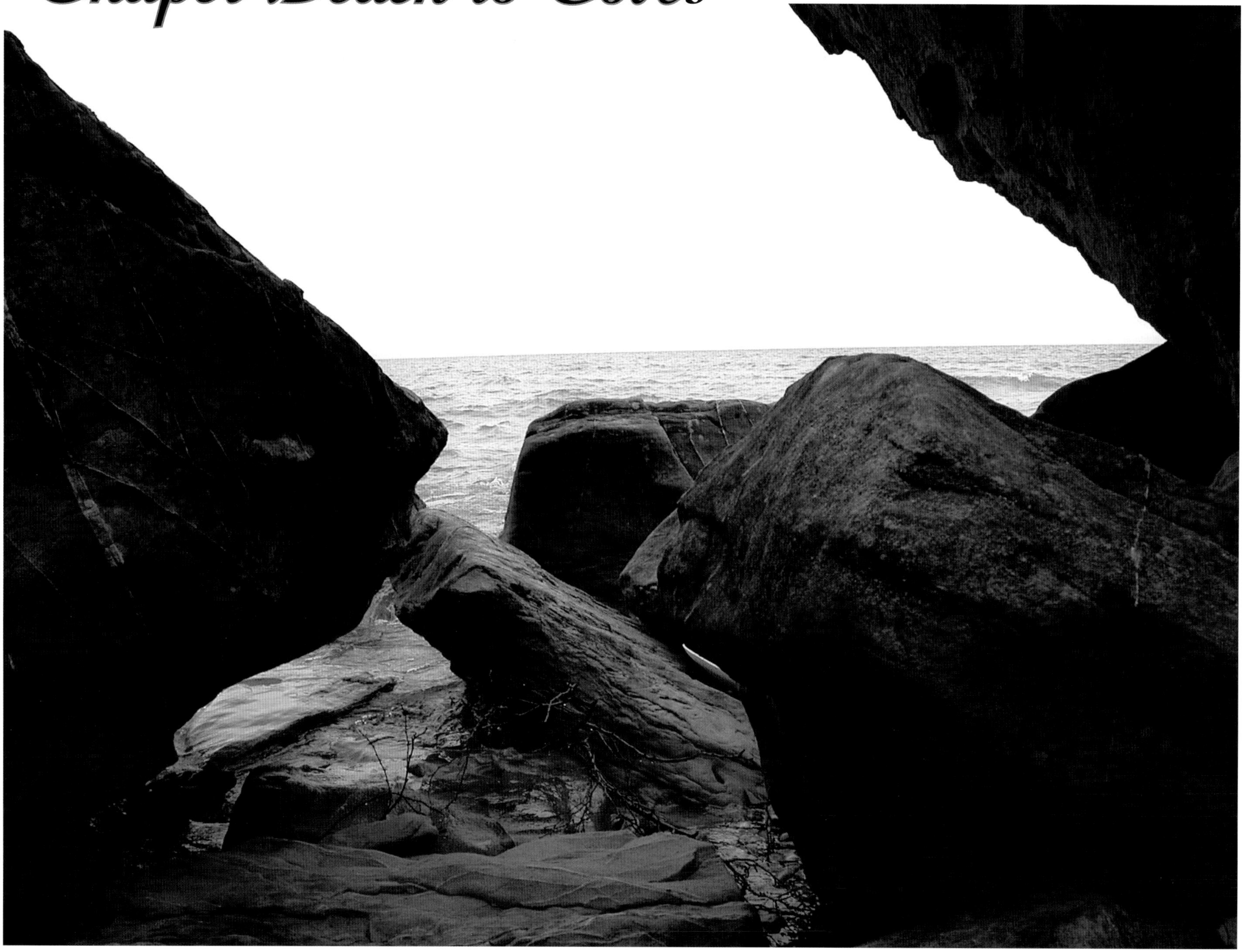

The Trail from Chapel Beach to Coves takes you from the cliffs section of Pictured Rocks to the beach section. This 3.5 mile hike curves along the top of the cliffs once more and then takes you down at a steep angle as the cliffs decrease in height. On this trail, you will be treated to several stunning views of the lake through the trees. A side trail will take you to the top of Spray Falls. These falls are best viewed from the water however.

Once you reach Coves backcountry campsite, you can choose to continue on the Lakeshore Trail, walk on Twelvemile Beach, or leave the lakeshore and turn inland to the Beaver Basin.

Beaver Basin

The Beaver Basin area consists of Beaver Lake, Little Beaver Lake, Little Beaver Campground, Beaver Basin Overlook, two backcountry campsites, and several miles of hiking trail loops.

Beaver Lake, at about 800 acres, is the largest inland lake in the park. It is a very popular boating and fishing lake, home to bass, pike, perch, walleye, trout, salmon and splake. Access to the lake is through Little Beaver Lake which borders the campground and boat launch.

You can park at the Beaver Basin Overlook, which provides an impressive view over the tree tops all the way to Lake Superior, and hike 2 miles down to Beaver Lake. Or you can park at the main trailhead near the campgound. From here, you can either hike around both lakes, or follow the trail along Beaver Creek 1.5 miles out to Lake Superior. Don't miss the White Pine Trail which is a short self-guided interpretive trail.

No matter which trail you take, you will be treated to a pleasant, easy hike through mixed hardwoods and conifers, with gorgeous lake views and access to several beaches.

Coves to Hurricane River

From Coves to Hurricane River stretches 12 miles of beach. The Lakeshore Trail is a wide sandy path through the woods, sometimes dense conifer and hardwoods, that parallels the beach and gives you wonderful glimpses of the lake. Many people prefer to leave the trail at this point and walk the beach instead.

There are many backcounty campgrounds along the trail in this area and of course, Twelvemile Beach campground, one of the most popular developed camping areas in the Park. Along the waters edge, Twelvemile beach is a rock hunter's paradise. Thousands of stones (quartz, jasper, chert, basalt, and even agate) litter the beach. The National Lakeshore does not permit the stones to be taken from the beach, but looking at all the magnificent colors can while away a lazy summer afternoon.

Hurricane River gathers speed as it approaches Lake Superior. It races under the bridge at the Hurricane River Campground and spills into the lake, cutting a channel through the beach. Fisherman like to try their luck at catching salmon in the spring and several types of trout year round. There is a picnic area and a wide sandy beach.

The Au Sable Light Station is just a short walk from the campground down an old road. The road, now only open to foot traffic, parallels the lake and gives you stunning glimpes of the red rock shale that sits just a few feet under the water. This rock reef extends a mile out into Lake Superior and has caused many shipwrecks. Several paths from the road will take you down to the beach where you can view shipwreck remains still located on the beach.

Au Sable Light Station

The Au Sable Light Station was built in 1874 to warn ships of the rock reef. A small light, powered by solar panels still works today. Interpretive panels and wayside exhibits surround the light station and provide a detailed history of the area. In the summer months, the National Park Service gives tours of the lighthouse and you can go up into the tower and look for miles in all directions.

Au Sable to Log Slide

As you leave the Au Sable Light Station heading east, the Lakeshore Trail takes you 3.5 miles to the Log Slide Overlook. This section of the trail is one of the most scenic in the park because it stays fairly close to the lake and provides you with many glimpes of the dunes looming 300 feet tall in the distance. Along the first part of the trail, you will encounter many rocky coves and inlets that you can explore. You could spend an entire day in one of these private beaches, listening to the waves roll in, rock hunting, and admiring the sunlight change the color of the dunes. About half way, the trail turns steeply up and takes you on top of the first dunes. As you look back, you can see the Au Sable Lighthouse towering majestically over the pines. As you look forward, the dunes stretch before you endlessly into the horizon. It is a truly spectacular view and worth the arduous climb to get there.

The Log Slide is aptly named and is a throwback to the logging days when Lake Superior was a throughfare for large amounts of timber. A wooden platform juts out over the dune and gives you a good view of the chute that was once used to move logs to the lake quickly. Wayside exhibits provide history of the area and the logging camps. Picnic tables and water are provided near the parking area.

Log Slide to Grand Sable Falls

The dunes stretch 8 miles from the Log Slide overlook to Grand Sable Falls located at the east end of the park. The Lakeshore Trail from here, however, mostly takes you though the thick hardwood forest on the back side of the dunes. This is an excellent place to view wildflowers in the spring. There are a few places where you can access the dunes along the way and there are trails from the Sable Falls parking area. Once on top of the dunes, you will see windswept panoramas of dune grasses and berries. The colors are rich and vibrant and the winds are fierce.

If you follow the trail, it will eventually cross H-58 and take you past Grand Sable Lake. This large lake is popular for both fishing and boating. Picnic tables and restrooms are located on the east shore. About a mile from the lake, the trail will take you to the Grand Sable Visitor Center, which is open from Memorial Day to Labor Day.

A short mile from the Grand Sable Visitor Center, the Lakeshore Trail ends at the Grand Sable Falls parking area. A short path will take you to the wooden stairs and viewing platform, where you can watch the Sable Falls cascade into Sable Creek and flow into Lake Superior. There are picnic tables, water and restrooms available in this area and many hiking trails to explore.

An opposite path will take you onto the dunes where you can follow several trails in the sand. *Use caution when hiking on the dunes, it is easy to become disoriented and lose direction. It is also easy to roll down a steep ravine and have trouble climbing back up.*

By Shoreline...

Pictured Rocks National Lakeshore

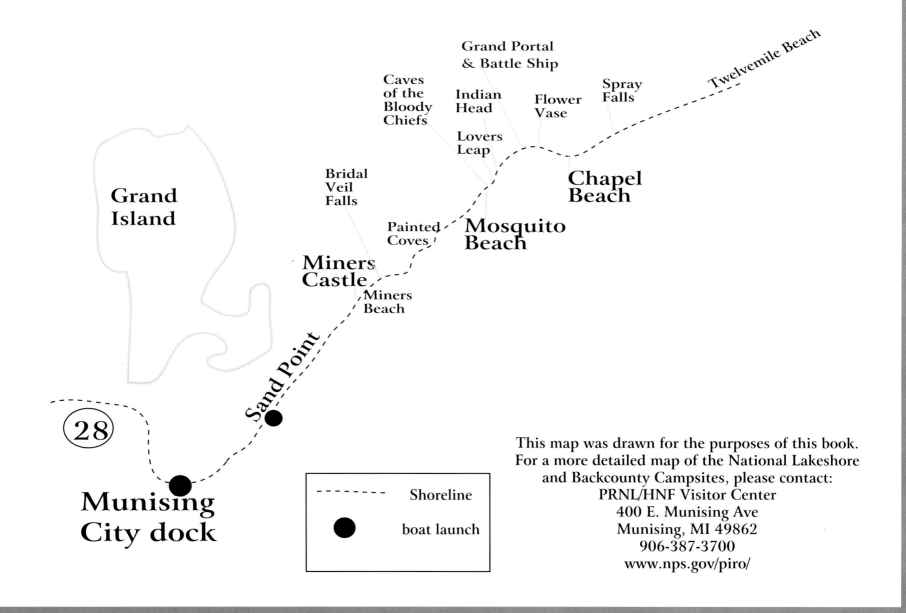

Grand Portal
& Battle Ship

Caves
of the
Bloody
Chiefs

Indian
Head

Spray
Falls

Flower
Vase

Twelvemile Beach

Lovers
Leap

Bridal
Veil
Falls

Chapel
Beach

**Grand
Island**

Painted
Coves

**Mosquito
Beach**

**Miners
Castle**

Miners
Beach

Sand Point

28

**Munising
City dock**

Shoreline

boat launch

This map was drawn for the purposes of this book.
For a more detailed map of the National Lakeshore
and Backcounty Campsites, please contact:
PRNL/HNF Visitor Center
400 E. Munising Ave
Munising, MI 49862
906-387-3700
www.nps.gov/piro/

From Munising Bay to Miners Castle, the lakeshore is fairly straight and low. The cliffs show only muted colors and no outstanding landmarks. It is interesting to note however, that here, where the shoreline is protected by Grand Island, trees and vegetation are plentiful, some growing down to the water's edge.

As you move along the shoreline, out of Grand Island's shadow, you will see that strong winds and waves have scoured almost all traces of plant life from the cliff's face.

Miners Castle

Bridal Veil Falls

   Miners Castle is really the true entrance to the Pictured Rocks shoreline. After you pass Miners Beach, the cliffs become more picturesque and the colors truely start to glow.

   Bridal Veil Falls is the first landmark after Miners Castle. Its name comes from the lacy quality of the water as it gently trickles down the cliff face. This waterfall is greatly affected by the amount of rainfall received and the heat of the summer. In hot dry periods, the water flow completely stops.

Painted Coves

As you pass Bridal Veil Falls, the cliffs become taller and the geological layers more pronounced. For the next three miles of shoreline until you reach Mosquito Beach, you will be treated to a breathtaking array of colors and patterns. It is here that you can see the minerals seeping through the porous sandstone. As was mentioned in the introduction, copper creates the blue/green hue, manganese gives the black stain, and iron brings the rust/brown bleeds. These minerals combine with white, light grey, cream and dark red rock to create the many shades of Pictured Rocks.

This area is generally known as painted coves. The shoreline dips in and out, dotted with small caves and inlets. This section is one of the most heavily kayaked areas of the Lakeshore. Caution should be used by all boaters, however, as there is nowhere to land in this area if the lake turns rough.

Caves of the Bloody Chiefs

As you pass Mosquito Beach, you will see a series of caves along the waterline. Stained in dramatic dark reds, yellows, and browns, these caves have become known as the Caves of the Bloody Chiefs. Folklore states that Indian warlords would put their enemies in these caves from which there was no escape. Days would pass while the prisoners waited for the lake to wash in and drown them. Gory legends aside, these caves are stunning in the early evening, when the setting sun deepens the colors and casts ominous shadows.

Lovers Leap

It seems all storm prone cliffs have a point called Lovers Leap. The first arch that juts out into the water is Pictured Rocks' version. However, there are no official records of anyone ever having jumped to their death from this point.

As you pass Lovers Leap, you will see many areas of the shoreline where rock formations have given into the harsh conditions and fallen into the lake. These rocks now tend to provide a buffer to the cliff wall, and plant life can once again find a foothold.

Before you reach Indian Head, you will pass the Rainbow Cave. This cave not only gets its name from the wide range of colors found on the rock, but also from the fact that water continuously drips in the cave causing what looks like a rain shower.

Rainbow Cave

Indian Head

Grand Portal

Grand Portal is named for the large arched passageway through the rock. Until recently, boats could safely pass though the stone tunnel. However, in the late 1990's part of the roof collapsed making the opening impossible to pass through.

Battleship Row

As you round Grand Portal, you will instantly see Battleship Row, so called because of the several large rock formations that jut out one after another. Each point looks like the bow of a great ship heading out to sea.

In between each of these points are beautiful coves like the one pictured above. The water can be deep enough to fit a large boat such as a Pictured Rocks Boat Cruises' boat. In some places, you can get so close, you can almost touch the rock.

Flower Vase

Can you see the flower vase in the picture to the left? There are many wonderful formations to be found along the shoreline, too numerous to show in this book. Like clouds, no two rocks look exactly alike and you can find faces and objects everywhere you look.

As you pass the flower vase, you will see Chapel Beach. As we mentioned earlier in this book, Chapel Beach is a very popular spot so you will most likely see many people wandering the area. On the east end of the beach, Chapel River flows into Lake Superior. From the water, you have an excellent view of Chapel Rock and the tree that proudly sits on top.

Chapel Area

Spray Falls

Spray Falls is best viewed from the water. This powerful waterfall can not be appreciated from the Lakeshore Trail unless you lean dangerously far over the edge of the cliff.

East of Spray Falls, the cliffs taper off into Twelvemile Beach and beyond that, the dunes rise 300 feet from the water line. Although these areas are also beautiful to see from the water, our trip by shoreline ends here.

It is at this point that the Pictured Rocks Boat Cruises turn around and head back to Munising Bay. The cliffs section of Pictured Rocks is by far the most popular section for boaters due to the unique and fascinating stone features and colors.

We hope that you have enjoyed this glimpse of Pictured Rocks from the land and from the water. You can explore this National Lakeshore many times and always come away with a different experience. Every season and time of day brings out different colors in the lake, in the sand, in the trees, and in the stone.

We hope that you will cherish the special beauty of this Lakeshore and take home special memories of your own.

Photo Credits

Cover: Pictured Rocks Shoreline Featuring Lovers Leap as taken from the trail just west of Mosquito Beach. *Photo by Autumn Jauck © 2004*

i: Red Trillium, a rare and protected wildflower species found at the lakeshore. *Photo by Laura Pederson © 2004*

pg. 1: Sunlight in a hardwood stand along the trail to Chapel Falls. *Photo by Autumn Jauck © 2003*

pg. 3: Painted Coves taken from a boat along the Pictured Rocks Shoreline. *Photo by Autumn Jauck © 2004*

pg. 4: Grand Sable Dunes just east of Log Slide. *Photo by Laura Pederson © 2004*

pg. 5: Bottom right photo is the Lakeshore Trail through the woods between Miners Castle and Mosquito Beach. Upper right photo is the beach at Sand Point. *Photos by Autumn Jauck © 2004*

pg. 7: Photo on the left is large driftwood on Sand Point beach. Photo on right is a shot of the Lake Superior stones underwater along the Sand Point Beach. *Photos by Autumn Jauck © 2004*

pg. 8: Lake Superior in Winter, standing on Sand Point Beach looking east towards Pictured Rocks shoreline. *Photo by Autumn Jauck © 2005*

pg. 9: View of Grand Island National Recreation Area from the west side of Sand Point Beach. *Photo by Autumn Jauck © 2004*

pg. 10: Photo on the left is the Lakeshore Trail between Sand Point and Miners Castle. Photo on the right is Jasper Falls, located half way between Sand Point and Miners Castle. *Photos by Autumn Jauck © 2004*

pg. 11: Full page photo is Miners Castle in the spring. *Photo by Laura Pederson © 2004* - Small photo is Miners Castle in February. *Photo by Autumn Jauck © 2005*

pg. 12: Photo on the left is close up of Miners Castle taken from wooden overlook. *Photo by Laura Pederson © 2004* – Photo on the right shows an oncoming storm through the rock turrets on top of Miners Castle. *Photo by Autumn Jauck © 2004*

pg. 13: Miners Beach. *Photo by Autumn Jauck © 2003*

pg. 14: Photo on the left is a kayaker at the east end of Miners Beach. Photo in the middle is a closeup of blueberries found at Miners Beach. *Photos by Autumn Jauck © 2004* - Photo on the right shows Miners Falls. *Photo by Laura Pederson © 2004*

pg. 15: East end of Miners Beach at sunset. *Photo by Autumn Jauck © 2004*

pg. 16: Photo on the left is the view of the shoreline from the Lakeshore trail between Miners Beach and Mosquito Beach. *Photo by Autumn Jauck © 2004* - Photo on the right is Mosquito Falls. *Photo by Laura Pederson © 2004*

pg. 17: Standing on Mosquito Beach looking east at the shoreline as it curves around. *Photo by Autumn Jauck © 2004*

pg. 18: Top left photo is a view of the shoreline looking east from Mosquito Beach. Bottom left photo is a frog found on Mosquito Beach. Photo on the right is a view of Mosquito Beach looking west. *Photos by Autumn Jauck © 2003*

pg. 19: View of shoreline just east of Mosquito Beach. *Photo by Laura Pederson © 2004*

Photo on the right by Autumn Jauck © 2005